ALABASTER

Library of Congress Cataloging-in-Publication Data is available upon request.
Library of Congress Control Number:
ISBN: 9781952357534

FSC
www.fsc.org
MIX
Paper | Supporting
responsible forestry
FSC® C013123

Printed in Italy by Graphicom S.p.A.

Contact
hello@alabasterco.com
www.alabasterco.com

Alabaster Co explores the intersection of creativity, beauty, and faith.
Founded in 2016. Based in Los Angeles.

The Advent Devotional

Listening to the Wonder of the Christmas Season

TABLE OF CONTENTS

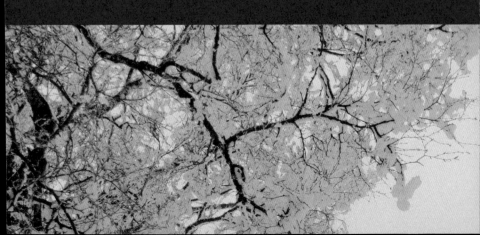

INTRODUCTION

The air is crisp; the twinkle lights are starting to be put out, and the trees are beginning to be brought in. Christmastime is upon us once again. Of all the markers of the season, perhaps the most ubiquitous is the music. Christmas songs have an extraordinary power to transport us to moments long past, connect us with loved ones, and invoke a sense of warmth and wonder to the season. Song is a means to discover and experience God—and, as we look at the history of song in the Bible, we find it can become a foundation for our Advent journey.

Advent is the name given to the four weeks leading up to Christmas. Advent, derived from the Latin *adventus* meaning "coming", is a time of remembrance and anticipation before the celebration of Jesus' birth. It invites us to enter into the Christmas season with intention, marking the passage of time and pausing to reflect and give thanks.

It is a tradition that echoes back to the expectancy that hung over the world ahead of the very first Christmas, as newlyweds awaited the birth of their child and magi charted the stars. And it is here that the first recorded Christmas songs rang out. Perhaps not as familiar as carols on our holiday playlists, these melodies have woven their way into the very fabric of our Christmas traditions all the same. Sacred harmonies that have reverberated through centuries, exploring the meaning and impact of the miracle of Jesus' birth.

This book invites us to experience these four biblical Christmas songs—the Song of Mary, the Song of Zechariah, the Song of the Angels, and the Song of Simeon—afresh and ruminate on how we can bring the wonder and beauty of this season into our daily lives. Each week begins with a reading from Scripture grounding us in the lyrics of each song. Following each passage, we offer a contemplative reading alongside imagery designed to inspire and encourage us. Finally, each chapter includes three reflection sections, exploring central ideas with responsive prompts that invite us to carry our insights with us into our week.

May this book be a companion on your journey through the Advent season, guiding you through the hushed whispers of anticipation and the crescendo of jubilation. Let the songs of Christmas lead us ever deeper into the awe-inspiring mystery of Emmanuel, God with us.

Week 1

The Song of Mary

Read

Full Reading: Luke 1:26-56

"Mary responded, 'Oh, how my soul praises the Lord. How my spirit rejoices in God my Savior! For he took notice of his lowly servant girl, and from now on all generations will call me blessed. For the Mighty One is holy, and he has done great things for me. He shows mercy from generation to generation to all who fear him. His mighty arm has done tremendous things! He has scattered the proud and haughty ones. He has brought down princes from their thrones and exalted the humble. He has filled the hungry with good things and sent the rich away with empty hands. He has helped his servant Israel and remembered to be merciful. For he made this promise to our ancestors, to Abraham and his children forever.'" — Luke 1:46-55

The Advent season is a time for reminiscing and retelling. Each year, as we await the coming of Christmas, we gather around and share all the best family stories, photos, and home videos. And while there is always space for new traditions, most of our focus is on what has come before us, remembering things that have made us smile in years past.

One of our most enduring traditions are the carols and hymns of the season. As the holidays approach, we sing familiar songs over and over, cherishing our favorite lyrics and voices in the comforting way that this time of year invites. Music has a unique ability to connect different people and generations. Well-known songs form a shared language between us, with common stories, feelings, and sentiments linking us together.

This community, built over song, was also part of first-century Jewish culture as significant stories were retold and passed down through song. Our modern understanding of the significance of songs is not all that different—they are a way for us to express more emotions in fewer words with a depth of sound to convey what lyrics alone cannot. Songs remain a poetic way to share our stories.

Within the first few verses of the Gospel of Luke, Mary gives voice to a song, also known as the Magnificat, that sets the tone for much of the story that is about to unfold. Pregnant and overjoyed, Mary's song offers praise to God for the story being told through her life. She gives voice to the knowledge that as a result of what God is doing in her life, "from now on all generations will call [her] blessed, for the Mighty One has done great things for [her]".[1] Another translation reads: "All the people who ever shall be will call me the happiest of women!".[2]

Mary is still human—she is just as unsure of how the story will develop as she is of who the child growing within her will become, but her reflection in this moment reveals steadfast confidence in what God is doing in partnership with her. Her song rings true with glad and hopeful praise in anticipation of what is to come. She is an instrument of the fulfillment of God's promises for all generations, just as her song has continued to be a reminder for generations after her.

Mary's song continues to be comforting as we seek hope in our own uncertainty. As God moved through the birth of Christ, Mary got to witness and praise, singing this song over and over and treasuring and ruminating on the memories in her heart. The appeal of Christmas is the same for us—we seek comfort and hope as we anticipate the continual fulfillment of God's plan for Creation.

What can we carry with us from a song so powerful that we join in the words of this young mother 2,000 years ago, repeating them year after year as Advent approaches? Awe and joy—these are the qualities Mary intertwined with her praise; together, they set the tone for much of the Advent season. Hundreds of our carols and songs mimic the tone of a joyful young mother, awed by the story God is telling through her life. There is a wonder to Christmas that we seek to capture through music; a sense that in entering into this season we are bearing witness to something life-changing.

We rejoice as light breaks over a too-dark world and dare to hope that the transformation God intends for the world will extend to us too. Later, after Mary gives birth to Jesus, she "treasured up all these things and pondered them in her heart".[3] Like many mothers, perhaps she continued to sing these same words of praise over her son long after the lullaby was needed, as she watched the refrain she vocalized become more and more true.

With that heart posture, may the words we sing and the stories we share ring more true to the person of God this year and in all our years to come. Carrying an attitude of joy, may we find hope and comfort as we watch and anticipate the actions of the God who is with us.

REFLECTION ONE: ON HOPE

Whether we are facing adversity, coping with uncertainty, or needing inspiration for what's to come, hope is an essential part of what it means to be human. Hope gives us the courage to dream; it powers our belief that tomorrow can be something better than today, and it gives us the resilience to overcome anything. Mary's song invites us into hope. It reveals we can be people who, through a posture of awe and joy, find hope in the continued promises of God. The story of God is not finished.

RESPOND

1. In what areas of your life do you find cultivating hope the most challenging? How can you invite God into those areas?
2. Are there certain daily routines or rhythms you can create that will help generate hope?
3. Consider the role of community in your hope journey. How can you seek the help of others in finding hope?

Further Readings on Hope:
The Story of Ruth – *Ruth 1-4*
The Story of Joseph – *Genesis 37-50*
The Story of Shadrach, Meshach, and Abednego – *Daniel 3*

REFLECTION TWO: ON PARTNERSHIP WITH GOD

There are times in our lives when God feels too abstract or too distant and we forget that God wants to have an active and intimate relationship with us. Just as God revealed the promises of Emmanuel through Mary, God wants to reveal the good things of life—healing, peace, Shalom, and love—through us. In the process, we are more than just vessels for God's will; we are active partners in shaping a better world for all of humanity. Partnership is an honor we all get to experience.

RESPOND

1. Reflect on a time when you experienced tangible power and guidance from God. What did you learn? How did it make you feel? How can you use that experience to guide you towards more partnership with God today?

2. Consider areas in your life where it is difficult to "partner" with God. What might be hindering your ability to let go of control and enter into collaboration?

3. How are you being invited to reveal God's Shalom (peace) today? How are you being invited to help heal and love those around you?

Further Readings on Partnership with God:

The Story of Lydia – *Acts 16:11-15*

The Story of Moses – *Exodus 3-4*

The Story of the Great Commission – *Matthew 28:18-20*

REFLECTION THREE: ON GENERATIONS

Mary understood her song was not just for her and those around her: it is for generations before her and for generations to come. How often do we think about our story in the context of those who came before us and those who will inherit the earth after us? Mary's song reveals a deep understanding that we are all connected to one another, and to those past, present, and yet to come. We are invited to reflect on our lives against the backdrop of this intergenerational reality.

RESPOND

1. Reflect on those who have come before you. How have they shaped you into who you are today? How can you honor what they have done for you?

2. Reflect on the role you might have on generations after you. How is your life serving as inspiration and encouragement to live into the type of goodness God intends for us?

3. Consider the different generations present in your community—how can you foster stronger cross-generational relationships, understanding that all generations have a seat at the table of God?

Further Readings on Generations:

The Story of Liberation for the Israelites – *Exodus 1-14*

The Story of Timothy – *1 Timothy 1:2, 2 Timothy 1:5*

The Story of the Early Church – *Acts 2:42-47*

The Song
of Zechariah

Read

Full Reading: Luke 1:5-25; 57-80

"Then his father, Zechariah, was filled with the Holy Spirit and gave this prophecy:

'Praise the Lord, the God of Israel, because he has visited and redeemed his people. He has sent us a mighty Savior from the royal line of his servant David, just as he promised through his holy prophets long ago. Now we will be saved from our enemies and from all who hate us. He has been merciful to our ancestors by remembering his sacred covenant—the covenant he swore with an oath to our ancestor Abraham. We have been rescued from our enemies so we can serve God without fear, in holiness and righteousness for as long as we live. And you, my little son, will be called the prophet of the Most High, because you will prepare the way for the Lord. You will tell his people how to find salvation through forgiveness of their sins. Because of God's tender mercy, the morning light from heaven is about to break upon us, to give light to those who sit in darkness and in the shadow of death, and to guide us to the path of peace.'"

— *Luke 1:67-79*

Sometimes we lose our voice at Christmas. The unexpected happens, and suddenly, our breath gets taken away. Life-altering news that we can hardly believe comes to us, and we are left silent. Muted. We can't find any words.

So it was for a man named Zechariah, an aging but faithful priest who had been waiting all his life for a child with his wife, Elizabeth. When the angel Gabriel finally tells Zechariah he will have a son, Zechariah can hardly believe it; after all, he and Elizabeth are quite old and had been waiting a long time! He was unprepared for the news that everything he had been waiting for—for which he had always hoped—was about to take place at last. He struggled to believe that what he was hearing could possibly be true.

It can be easier to expect disappointment instead of fulfillment. As the days turn into weeks and weeks turn into months and months turn into years, with nothing changing for the better, we can learn to settle for what we have rather than keep hoping for the best. And when the announcement of a turning point comes, it can be challenging to look beyond all our questions and release the hesitations to which we've grown accustomed.

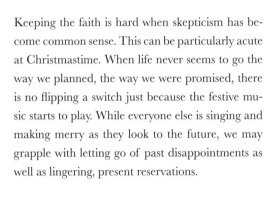

Keeping the faith is hard when skepticism has become common sense. This can be particularly acute at Christmastime. When life never seems to go the way we planned, the way we were promised, there is no flipping a switch just because the festive music starts to play. While everyone else is singing and making merry as they look to the future, we may grapple with letting go of past disappointments as well as lingering, present reservations.

Zechariah is left dumbstruck by his doubts. His reticence ends up turning into a pregnant pause as the soon-to-be father of a great prophet—of one who will be like "a voice crying in the wilderness" heralding humanity's salvation—is hushed by divine decree.[4] Zechariah emerges speechless—unable to say anything about what he has been told. Instead, for nine months and eight days, he gets to sit back and watch it all begin to unfold.

This heavenly imposed silence could be viewed as a rebuke. But it is better perceived as a gift, a blessing. For when we grow tired of waiting, we often adopt mindsets and postures that limit our reception to the possibilities breaking on the horizon. Getting stuck in the noise of our own heads often leaves little room for catching the vision of something bigger taking shape before us. The quiet enables us to listen and observe what we don't—what we can't—normally hear and see.

Learning to be still, we come to know our Creator is God. Not some distant, aloof deity who arbitrarily makes their presence known now and then, but the God who never stops laboring to heal and reshape all creation towards full, abundant, and everlasting life. As we enter rather than resist the stillness and the quiet that comes upon us in our fear and confusion, we are able to perceive the God who continues to work even in the midst of our disbelief.

Zechariah's lull eventually results in his transformation. Something changes within him. Previous apprehensions are eclipsed by his comprehension of past blessings. Old arguments and uncertainties are lifted by a growing awareness and anticipation of what God is birthing before his eyes. Eventually, with the birth of his son, Zechariah's mouth is opened. His tongue is loosened. Protest becomes praise as the first words out of his mouth are a blessing, a song.

What Zechariah sings is the song that remains the same. First authored by our Creator, it is an ancient melody we need to remember and learn to sing anew in what sometimes feels like the yawning gap between promise and fulfillment. It is the heavenly chorus of God's longstanding history of deliverance and redemption. A song that goes beyond mere words to become flesh—God with and for us in the person of Jesus Christ. A song that solidifies and signifies Zechariah's (and our own) transformation.

Ultimately, Zechariah finds his voice. Likewise, we are invited to find ours—to plunge through our own moments of silence and doubt and disappointments—and to come out the other side transformed. We, too, may end up finding a song: proclaiming the love and mercies of God that are present, not just at Christmas, but every morning.

REFLECTION ONE: ON SILENCE

Zechariah's temporary loss of speech allowed him to reflect and contemplate the miraculous events unfolding in his life. In the same way, silence allows all of us—in a world so inundated with noise and stimuli—to look inward and reflect on the good news of God. More than just an absence of sound, silence is a posture and a way of being; a choice on how to live that aligns with what God intends for all of us.

RESPOND

1. The world can be a distracting place: what do you need to do and where do you need to go in order to create a space for silence?

2. Reflect on the times when you find silence uncomfortable. What might be the underlying reasons for this discomfort? How can you go to God in the midst of this?

3. Consider the value of silence in relationships and community. How can silence create space for better listening, understanding, and empathy toward one another?

Further Readings on Silence:

The Story of Elijah – *1 Kings 19:9-18*

The Story of Jesus in the Wilderness – *Matthew 4:1-11*

The Story of Jesus Silencing the Storm – *Mark 4:35-41*

REFLECTION TWO: ON DOUBT & DISAPPOINTMENT

Like Zechariah, we are all subject to moments of doubt and disappointment. Christmastime, perhaps more than most seasons, makes us keenly aware of the ways in which we feel life has fallen short of our hopes and dreams. In these moments, we are invited to adopt a posture similar to Zechariah. By surrendering our doubts to God and trusting in His plans, we open ourselves to the possibility of a transformed faith, where disappointment gives way to divine fulfillment.

RESPOND

1. Reflect on a time in your life you were faced with doubt and disappointment. How did God help you in those moments?

2. Examine your response when faced with disappointment: Do you withdraw? Become defensive or controlling? How can you deal with disappointment in a healthy way?

3. Consider the community around you and how they might help you through times of doubt and disappointment. Who can you go to? Who can you be open to?

Further Readings on Doubt & Disappointment:
The Story of Thomas – *John 20:24-29*
The Story of Martha, Mary, and Lazarus – *Luke 10:38-42; John 11:1-44*
The Story of Peter Walking on Water – *Matthew 14:22-33*

REFLECTION THREE: ON TRANSFORMATION

Ultimately, Zechariah's life is transformed: through his silence, through his doubt, through his disappointment, by the birth of his son, John the Baptist. His life is so transformed that he writes a song, sharing gratitude and prophesying on the role his son will take in the larger story of God. There are moments in our lives, too, when who we once were is no longer who we are. We, too, have moments of transformation. In these times, how do we respond to what God is doing? What song are we invited to sing? How are we invited to remember our stories of change?

RESPOND

1. In what ways has God transformed you? Reflect on your life: 1 year ago, 5 years ago, 10 years ago. How were you transformed along the way?

2. How did you memorialize moments of transformation? Consider activities—singing songs, giving thanks, celebrating—that honor transformation.

3. How can you invite others into your transformation story? Likewise, when you see others being transformed how can you recognize and commemorate their transformation?

Further Readings on Transformation:

The Story of the Woman at the Well – *John 4:1-42*
The Story of Saul's Conversion – *Acts 9:1-19*
The Story of Nicodemus – *John 3:1-21*

Week 3

The Song of
the Angels

Read

Full Reading: Luke 2:8-20

"Suddenly, the angel was joined by a vast host of others—the armies of heaven—praising God and saying, 'Glory to God in highest heaven, and peace on earth to those with whom God is pleased.'" — Luke 2:13-14

With each passing year, the world experiences the groanings of conflict. Peace is eroded by a culture of division, injustice, and destruction. We sing of peace on earth and goodwill once the holiday season approaches but seldom do we extol the same sentiments year round. Christmas is more than a temporary season of wonderment, peace, and festivities. Christmas is the forever promise to this weary world that peace will be victorious and that darkness and conflict is the true temporary season. Christ's light prevails over the darkness every day, not just during Christmas.

That first Christmas, the angels filled the fields with a thunderous song, declaring Glory to God for such a momentous birth that would change the trajectory of the world. That promise of peace is the praise song that the angels proclaimed to the shepherds on the night when Jesus was born. Not to royalty or high officials, but to shepherds, whom society deemed lowly and unclean. Shepherds, though rebuffed and uncouth, were met in the field, where they made their livelihood, where they spent their lives. An ordinary field, not a lavish court or concert hall. An open space that held no boundaries, no fencing of private property. The promise fulfilled by Jesus' birth was not withheld from anyone, anywhere.

The promise of peace meets us where we are, with no criteria to be met, no status needed. The song of the angels rings out as we give glory to God for peace that is given freely, even on the days when we feel we do not deserve it. Moreover, peace is freely given to others even when we feel *they* do not deserve it. We do not need a season of practiced merriment, of displayed joy, of decorated peace. Even when the darkness of this world threatens to close in around us, Jesus' birth reminds us that God's plans never fail. That, even when everything seems consumed by chaos, the peace of Jesus tethers us to the ultimate plan to restore everything back to God. We can rejoice even when we are weary. We can rejoice even when the decorations come down because Jesus' birth is the triumph that promises good for all corners of the earth.

The angels' song is a melody of praise for a plan fulfilled, and it is our song too. Our very redemption was interwoven throughout the lives of God's people from the beginning, the plan to restore humanity back to God. Jesus' birth is more than the sign of peace to come, it is the converging of these threads of prophecy and promise throughout the

scriptures and our lives. The final tapestry, the fullness and wholeness of Shalom, will be on earth as it is in heaven. It is this song that unites the celestial and the earthly together with one voice declaring wonder and hope. A philharmonic crescendo that deafens the sounds of division and despair, as God reaches out to us.

REFLECTION ONE: ON PEACE

The angels' song illuminates God's desire to bring healing, restoration, and unity to a broken world, bridging the divide between heaven and earth. In contemplating this song, we are reminded of the transformative power of God's peace in our lives. It is an invitation to seek and experience the Shalom that Jesus offers—a peace that surpasses all understanding, permeating every aspect of our being. It is a peace that transcends circumstances, providing comfort, hope, and assurance no matter our circumstances.

RESPOND

1. How can you actively embrace and extend this peace to those around you? In what ways can you foster reconciliation, goodwill, and harmony in your relationships and communities?

2. In what areas of your life do you long for the transformative power of God's peace? How can you invite Jesus to bring healing, restoration, and wholeness to those areas? How does trusting God's peace enable you to navigate challenges and find hope and comfort?

3. What spiritual practices, such as prayer, meditation, or Scripture reading, can you incorporate to deepen your experience of peace during Advent?

Further Readings on Peace:

The Prayer of David – *Psalm 23*
The Story of God's Future Reign – *Micah 4:1-5*
The Story of Life in the Garden – *Genesis 1*

REFLECTION TWO: ON EXPECTATIONS AND PRECONCEPTIONS

The Song of the Angels and the audience of shepherds who witnessed it teach us that God's plans often disrupt our expectations. Humanity may have anticipated a royal birth in a palace, announced to the influential with pomp and grandeur. However, the angelic message shattered those preconceived ideas by revealing that the Savior was born in a humble manger in Bethlehem for all the world. We too are challenged to let go of our preconceived ideas and to embrace the unexpected and unconventional ways in which God reveals the Good News. It calls us to remain open, flexible, and receptive to divine leading, even when it breaks the social script.

RESPOND

1. The shepherds, often considered lowly and marginalized in society, were the recipients of the angels' glorious announcement. What does it look like to embrace a mindset that recognizes and affirms the value and worth of every person we encounter, irrespective of their background or social standing?

2. What are your expectations for God? How might your expectations prevent you from recognizing and receiving the unexpected ways in which God works?

3. Consider a recent experience where your expectations were shattered, and God worked in an unexpected way. What did you learn from that experience? How can you carry those lessons forward to cultivate a deeper trust and openness to God's plans for the future?

Further Readings on Expectations and Preconceptions:

The Story of David's Anointing – *1 Samuel 16:1-13*
The Story of Jacob and Esau – *Genesis 32:6-21; 33*
The Story of Peter and Cornelius – *Acts 10:1-34*

REFLECTION THREE: ON WORSHIP

The angels invite us to reflect on the nature and purpose of worship in our own lives. Worship is not merely an act of duty or obligation, but a response to the greatness and majesty of God. It is an expression of awe, reverence, and love for the Creator. As the angels demonstrate, it is not restricted to a particular location or circumstance. It is a way of life, permeating every aspect of our existence. May the Song of the Angels inspire us to approach worship with authenticity, fervor, and a deep sense of reverence, allowing it to color our lives and shape us into true worshippers who bring glory to God in all that we do.

RESPOND

1. Consider the daily moments and spaces of your routine. How can you incorporate worship as a way of life, aligning your thoughts, words, and actions with God's will and bringing glory to Him in all areas of your existence?

2. Reflect on any distractions or barriers that hinder your worship experience. Are there any attitudes, habits, or mindsets that need to be surrendered in order to cultivate a more genuine and focused worship? How can you intentionally remove those obstacles and create a space for unhindered worship in your life?

3. Reflect on the transformative aspect of worship. How has worship, in both communal settings and private moments, impacted your relationship with God and your perspective on life? How can you cultivate a deeper intimacy with God through regular and intentional times of worship?

Further Readings on Worship:

The Story of David's Dance of Worship – *2 Samuel 6*
The Story of the Woman Who Anointed Jesus – *Luke 7:36-50*
The Story of Paul and Silas – *Acts 16:16-34*

Week 4

The Song of Simeon

Read

Full Reading: Luke 2:21-35

"So when Mary and Joseph came to present the baby Jesus to the Lord as the law required, Simeon was there. He took the child in his arms and praised God, saying, 'Sovereign Lord, now let your servant die in peace, as you have promised. I have seen your salvation, which you have prepared for all people. He is a light to reveal God to the nations, and he is the glory of your people Israel!'" — Luke 2:27-32

We are approaching the culmination of Advent, this season of anticipation and preparation. We have been waiting for Christmas, imagining what gifts we might find under the tree. But what happens on the other side of Christmas? When Christ has come, when the presents are all unwrapped, and our dreams and longings have become reality, we're left to wonder what comes next.

Chronologically, the biblical song we reflect upon here—the Song of Simeon—was first sung well after the events of Christmas Eve. This melody comes 40 days after Jesus' birth as his parents bring him to be presented in the Temple. It may seem odd to consider such a passage in the lead-up to Christmas; most of us will have called it quits with the holiday carols long before February. And yet, there are few people whose stories are more in line with this season of waiting and anticipation than Simeon's.

A man of great faith and devotion, we are told that Simeon had been assured by the Holy Spirit that he would not die before he had seen the promised Savior. Luke writes that Simeon "was eagerly waiting" for Jesus. We have seen this kind of eager anticipation reflected in the other biblical Christmas songs we've considered throughout the season. Mary, Zechariah, and the heavenly angels all celebrate what God has done and look ahead with hope to what the birth of Jesus will mean. Simeon's song echoes Mary's declarations of God's faithfulness. He joins Zechariah's refrain of gratitude for God's preparation. He harmonizes with the angels in proclaiming hope for all the world.

But Simeon's song is not entirely reprisal. His alone of the four Advent hymns addresses God in the second person—"I have seen *your* salvation, which *you* have prepared for all people."[5] A simple detail on the surface, yet it denotes that for Simeon the emphasis is not just on what we sing, but also on who we sing to. Christmas comes and goes each year, but the miracle it celebrates is everlasting. We carry the song of Christmas in our hearts all through the year; Emmanuel is not confined to 25 days each December. God is with us always.

The joy of Christmas is not vague or unknowable. It is the personal unveiling of God's love for all the world, a redemptive and transformative chord that sets the world back into tune. Wrongs will be righted, darkness will be illuminated. Promises will come to pass.

It is hard to ignore our culture's predilection for consumption, particularly during this time of year. We are a people constantly on the move—always looking for more, always onto the next thing. Christmas sales bleed into New Year's blowouts as brands and storefronts direct our attention to the gifts we didn't receive, to the things we still yearn for. We chastise ourselves continually, wishing we were better—more impressive. We worry we are not enough.

In the midst of this, Simeon's song is one of satisfaction and contentment. The desires of his heart have been fulfilled and he is at peace. To join our voices with Simeon's is to see ourselves—our lives—not through the lens of what we may lack, but as reflections of God's goodness and mercy. Time spent waiting is not wasted, but instead, a posture of patience allows the gift of God's promises to unfold. Our weaknesses and struggles are not failings but reminders that our Creator is forever refining and strengthening us. Simeon's song is but a verse in the cosmic symphony the earth has been singing since its creation. It is an age-old chorus we were made to sing.

¹ Shout joyful praises to God, all the earth!
² Sing about the glory of his name!
  Tell the world how glorious he is.
³ Say to God, "How awesome are your deeds!
  Your enemies cringe before your mighty power.
⁴ Everything on earth will worship you;
  they will sing your praises,
  *shouting your name in glorious songs."*⁶

As we reflect on Simeon and the wonder of Christmas, we rediscover this ancient melody. The song that places our Creator at the center of all things and gratefully anticipates—celebrates—the promises of redemption. God's promises are always kept. The gift of Christmas is not conditional; withheld from the naughty and bestowed upon the nice. It is a comfort, a reassurance, an invitation to stop, give thanks, and share out of the blessings we have been given. May we be at peace.

REFLECTION ONE: ON PATIENCE

In a world that often promotes instant gratification, the story of Simeon reminds us that patience is a virtue worth cultivating. It invites us to lean on God, trust in divine promises, and wait with expectant hope for God's plans to unfold. Patience is not passive resignation but an active, hopeful stance that leans into God's faithfulness. Through Simeon's example, we are called to examine our own posture of patience—we are moved to cultivate a spirit of readiness and expectation and trust that God's timing is perfect.

RESPOND

1. How does Simeon's patient waiting challenge your own attitude towards waiting for God's promises to be fulfilled in your life? In what areas do you struggle with impatience, and how can Simeon's story inspire you to cultivate a patient and trusting heart?

2. Consider a time when you experienced delayed answers to prayers or unfulfilled desires. How did you respond in those moments? How can Simeon's example encourage you to trust in God's faithfulness, even when that timing differs from your own?

3. Think about the role of prayer in cultivating patience. How does consistent prayer and seeking God's guidance help you maintain a patient attitude? In what ways can prayer strengthen your faith and resilience during seasons of waiting?

Further Readings on Patience:
The Story of Hannah – *1 Samuel 1-2*
The Story of God's Patience with Jonah – *Jonah 1-4*
The Story of Esther – *Esther 4-10*

REFLECTION TWO: ON CONTENTMENT

Simeon's response upon seeing the infant Jesus reveals a deep sense of contentment. Contentment is not complacency or resignation, but rather an inner peace that comes from aligning our hearts with God's will and trusting in God's faithfulness. Simeon's contentment stemmed from his unwavering faith in God's promises, even during a time of waiting and uncertainty. In a world that often encourages us to seek happiness and satisfaction in external circumstances, Simeon's example reminds us that true contentment lies in the presence of God; the path to wholeness, to fulfillment, is found in our relationship with Jesus.

RESPOND

1. Reflect on moments in your own life when you have experienced true contentment. What were the circumstances surrounding those moments? How can you cultivate a deeper sense of contentment by recognizing and embracing the presence of God in your daily life?

2. In what ways do you find yourself being restless or discontented? How can the example of Simeon inspire you to embrace the present moment, trust in God's timing, and find contentment even in times of waiting or uncertainty?

3. Consider the impact of societal pressures and external influences on your pursuit of contentment. How can you release the burden of finding contentment in worldly achievements, possessions, or comparisons? How can you refocus your priorities and seek contentment in God's presence and promises?

Further Readings on Contentment:

The Story of Daniel – *Daniel 6*
The Story of Martha and Mary – *Luke 10:38-42*
The Parable of the Lilies in the Field – *Luke 12:22-34*

REFLECTION THREE: ON GRATITUDE

Gratitude is an attitude of the heart that acknowledges God's goodness, mercy, and love. It helps us recognize and appreciate the ways in which God works in our lives and the blessings bestowed upon us. As Simeon shows us, gratitude transforms our perspective, enabling us to see beyond our circumstances and focus on the faithfulness of our Creator. In his story, we find an invitation to cultivate a deeper sense of gratitude. We are reminded to pause and reflect on the ways in which God is at work in our lives for our good and how God has offered us hope in Jesus Christ.

RESPOND

1. How do you currently cultivate a grateful heart and acknowledge God's faithfulness in your life? Are there specific practices or habits you can incorporate to deepen your gratitude?

2. Explore the impact of gratitude on your relationships with others. How does expressing gratitude towards others strengthen your connections and foster a spirit of generosity and kindness? How can you cultivate a culture of gratitude in your interactions with family, friends, and colleagues?

3. Consider the role of gratitude in your life of faith. How does expressing gratitude to God deepen your relationship with Him? How might a grateful heart lead to a greater sense of awe, worship, and intimacy with our Creator?

Further Readings on Gratitude:

The Story of Jehoshaphat – *2 Chronicles 20*
The Story of the Ten Lepers – *Luke 17:11-19*
The Song of Moses and Miriam – *Exodus 15:1-21*

 ALABASTER

EMMA TWEITMANN
Head Writer & Chief Editor

SAMUEL HAN
Art Director

TYLER ZAK
Product Director

BRYAN YE-CHUNG
Co-Founder, Creative Director

BRIAN CHUNG
Co-Founder, Managing Director

WILLA JIN
Finance & Talent Director

EMALY HUNTER
Operations & Customer Experience Director

MINZI BAE
Senior Marketing Coordinator

ZACH MCKINLEY
Cover Image

WRITERS

Chris Tweitmann (The Song of Zechariah)

Emma Tweitmann (The Song of Simeon)

Mary Taylor (The Song of the Angels)

Sabrina Dawson (The Song of Mary)

PHOTOGRAPHERS

Bekah Wriedt

Fiona Cook

Heidi Parra

Jonathan Knepper

Kristen Hahn

Makito Umekita

Samuel Han

Sophia Hsin

Zach Mckinley

ENDNOTES

THE SONG OF MARY

1. Luke 1:48b-49, NIV.
2. Luke 1:48-49, PHILLIPS.
3. Luke 2:19, NIV.

THE SONG OF ZECHARIAH

4. Luke 1:19-20, NLT.

THE SONG OF SIMEON

5. Luke 2:31 NLT, italics added.
6. Psalm 66:1-4, NLT